Dropshipping E-Commerce Business Model 2020

A Step-by-Step Guide With The Latest Techniques On How To Start Building , Growing and Scaling Your Shopify and Online Store in No Time

Phil Ortiz

By reading this document, the reader agrees that under no circumstances is the author responsible for any losses, direct or indirect, which are incurred as a result of the use of information contained within this document, including, but not limited to, — errors, omissions, or inaccuracies.

Table of Contents

Introduction

Few things in life can be more exhilarating than starting and running your own profitable business. The independence, the flexibility, the competition — it is all a catnip for the natural entrepreneur. The first task in entrepreneurship is the identification of a market opportunity and acquiring the resources to fulfill it. In the current digital age, internet-based businesses are all the buzz. And the good thing about the internet is that it is here to stay. The world will continue to use the internet more and more, with the world getting smaller as globalization takes root.

We are already seeing the massive changes that the internet has brought to every area of business, as well as the massive opportunities that it has created. In just a few years, online businesses have started to overtake traditional ones, setting the pace for growth far beyond the old boundaries. We have also seen the impact of the internet on the retail sector where the massive hitherto untapped potential for online shopping launched online retailers like to the very forefront of retailing, beating the traditional stores in just a couple of years.

Today, there are hundreds of thousands of online stores selling every kind of product imaginable, e.g., food, furniture, books, toys, clothes, shoes, and a million other household and business products. However, there is still a huge demand for online shopping solutions, as well as some of the things people need cannot be supplied by the big players. In this thriving environment, concepts like dropshipping have taken off, empowering thousands of entrepreneurs to start their own businesses. With dropshipping, to be specific, an online store sells products without stocking them physically in their shops and buys them from a third party when the customer requests them and ships them.

In dropshipping, geographical and political borders are no longer a hindrance to business. People can buy and sell from and to people all over the world almost as easily as they can do that with individuals in their immediate neighborhood. Let's think about that with an example. Cathy, who lives in suburban Cape Town, wants a product that she has no idea how to find in her city. Or maybe she just wants to buy it online and save herself the hustle of going to the store, buying it, and transporting it all the way home. She could search online, find sellers with the lowest prices, and make an order. It could easily turn out that the dropshipping business from which she ordered is operated from Detroit, New York, London, or any other city in the whole world. The operator of that business then routes the order to a supplier from any city in the world (even Cape Town) and have them delivered to Cathy. Cathy pays the dropshipping company, which in turn pays the supplier and the delivery service.

The godfather of dropshipping is Shopify, a Canadian e-commerce company that offers traders with e-commerce platforms to run their online stores as well as point of sale systems. With Shopify, small online stores can organize for shipping, payments, marketing, and customer service tools all from one place. The availability of these systems has contributed massively to the explosion of small online stores selling niche products all over the world. Shopify is the biggest success story in the dropshipping environment, going as far as to become a strategic partner with Amz while at the same time inspiring thousands of other success stories.

So, now you will hear and see online stories about people making as much as $10,000 a day from their dropshipping businesses. These are enterprising businessmen and women who have identified niche markets and found the resources they have needed to exploit them. Luckily, there is no shortage of dropshipping support businesses offering various peripheries and proprietary software for a small fee, enabling these entrepreneurs to start out with a tiny fraction of the cost needed to start a traditional store. Not only have dropshipping entrepreneurs fulfilled customer needs and served thousands of satisfied customers, but they have also made thousands of passive income for themselves.

The stage is all set for enterprising business women and men to completely take over the world of retailing. As the small dropshipping businesses grow and master the art of selling conveniently to customers from every corner of the world, the dynamics of shopping will shift even further. It is common knowledge that superstores like Wal-Mart failed to capture the entire market because they could not command all the niche products. The same is true for the likes of Amz and Alibaba. The massive selling taking place there obscures the smaller niche products like anime paraphernalia. A dropshipping entrepreneur can then take up these products and offer them on their store, reaching people in the remotest part of the world just as easily as Alibaba or Amz.

In just a few years, the faint boundaries that exist today marking different jurisdictions will be no more as far as business is concerned. Dropshipping promises to globalize the retail markets much as Bitcoin and other cryptocurrencies are slowly globalizing the world currencies. As a prospecting business person, it is advisable to start positioning yourself to profit from the impending disruption to the low-volume retail section. And why shouldn't you? Dropshipping is one of the easiest businesses to set up and run. All the tools you need are available for free or at a small fee online, and you can operate it from anywhere in the world as long as you have an internet connection!

Chapter 1: Dropshipping 101

Simply defined, dropshipping is a business model that allows a store to sell products that they don't own, buy, and never touch. In dropshipping, the store is an execution agent that only buys a product from a third party once a customer makes a purchase. The main role of a dropshipper is to ensure that the product reaches the customer, which they accomplish remotely.

How Does It Work?

Dropshipping allows a business to enjoy all the benefits of retailing without suffering through all the hassle, such as stocktaking and inventory cost. Because you never own the stock you sell, you won't need thousands of dollars' worth of supplies to start up. Along with this, you will be freed up from the massive insurance, security, and maintenance costs that come with the actual stock on your shelves. Of course, because customers will never have to avail themselves physically to make a purchase, you don't need a physical location from which to run your business. The only thing you will need in dropshipping will be a computer and internet connection — maybe a desk, too — and you will be all set to go.

Pros and Cons

Dropshipping has many advantages over traditional retailing businesses. However, it is also fraught with challenges that make it a hassle to start and get it going as discussed below.

Pros

Low startup cost

The first and most obvious advantage of dropshipping is that it requires very little money to start. Everything in dropshipping is designed to leverage the internet to grant you with an easy, stress-free, and optimized investment opportunity.

Low-cost inventory

Dropshipping does not just allow you to start your business with the cheapest inventory possible. It also lets you to open your "store" with no inventory at all! All you have to do is find the customers, then the suppliers and delivery services will take care of everything. No need to get your hands dirty at all.

Low order fulfillment cost

Order fulfillment is the most expensive aspect of online businesses. Before getting the product loaded on the delivery truck, van, or bike, online stores have to conduct the tedious job of warehousing, tracking, labeling, packing, and finally, transporting. In dropshipping, the price of all these services is factored into the transaction. Whatever the customer pays, the supplier and delivery service's cut is factored in. You set your own margin and compete with other dropshippers for the limited number of customers.

Less risk of loss

Because you require no inventory and no premises to start, the risk of losing money is very minimal in dropshipping. In fact, the only starting costs associated with dropshipping are the marketing and promotion that you have to pay for to popularize your business. By identifying products that are already doing very well among other dropshippers, you can ride the wave and spend substantially less money with advertising because the groundwork will already be set.

Cons

No control over the process

The downside of having third parties fulfill the orders and deliver to your customer is that you have very little control over both. Any mistakes they make will reflect badly on you, even when you have little control and can hardly do anything about it.

Less profit

When traditional sellers buy their stock, they get discounted prices because they buy in bulk. Meaning, their profit margins are bigger. In dropshipping, the markup you can put on a product and remain profitable is very low. Therefore, you need to sell more products compared to traditional retailers to accumulate the same amount of profit.

High levels of conflict

In dropshipping, you have to juggle two different relationships at once to make it work- the customer and the supplier. If the supplier delivers the wrong product, damages the goods, or is late in their fulfillment of the order, the customer will berate you for something that you had very little control over. Talking with customers and suppliers over the phone or through texts and emails also denies you the opportunity to establish a personal relationship.

Budget

The budgetary needs for starting a dropshipping business on Shopify includes the cost of opening a merchant account with Shopify, starting a website, making store enhancements to optimize your platform for selling, and advertising your business to get customers.

To start a dropshipping business on Shopify, you will first have to open a paid Shopify account. The cheapest will cost you $29 a month and give you unlimited products, two staff accounts, full-time support, and hardware peripheral support, among other things. For an additional 50 bucks, you get five staff accounts, gift cards, professional report builders, and $0.2 less on in-person credit card rates. You will get the first 14 days free to set up and determine if you still want to continue with the paid plan.

The next item on the list is the acquisition of a domain name for your store. A dropshipping website needs to be professionally done and meet the high standards of e-commerce sites. With Shopify, you only need to pay $14 to get a domain. To boost this, you can open a dropshipping app with Oberlo for $29, gaining access to AliExpress as well. Another great app is Spocket, which connects you with dropshipping suppliers from all over the world. A free plan gives you a maximum of 24 products, but you will have to upgrade to a paid account to add more products to your store.

Enhancing your store increases your conversion rates and increases profitability. With a standard Shopify account, you cannot add bulk discounts, sale pop-ups, cross sales, or count-down timers for items on sale. Each of these enhancements cost between $19 and $30, but they will make your store a lot more profitable. You can choose to start with the discount ($19) and sale pop-ups (free) because they are more important. You can then add the rest as you go if you are on a budget when starting.

Marketing is the bane of every business. Marketers say that even the best product in the world would sell less than the worst product if the latter was better marketed. With dropshipping, the early days of a business are very crucial. You can't get those first customers that popularize your store unless you advertise. Use Google or Facebook ads — they are the most effective — to reach a very targeted demographic for maximum effectiveness. About $5-$10 per day should be enough. A reserve enough to cover the first two weeks (which is when most dropshippers start to make money) brings the total to about $105. However, if you follow the lessons in this book, you will find a product in massive demands and it may never come to this. You will probably be making a good profit by the second week and using the money to advertise.

Taking all these costs into consideration, the total budget for starting a dropshipping business comes in at around $200 if you take the 14 days free trial on Shopify and use Oberlo's paid service for your store. If you go with the Shopify free service and the free Spocket package, it comes down to about $170. Either way, the greatest expenditure is in the marketing department. This is quite in order because if you don't advertise, you will probably get no customers at all. It is better to commit to the process and risk failure than go with the $0 startup cost hogwash peddled in some quarters. The risk is well worth it if you are really committed.

Mindset

"You cannot succeed in anything if you don't have the right mindset." This is a quote every one of us must have encountered at one point. It is very true for dropshipping as well. You will not go far as a dropshipper if you don't take the time to develop the right mindset. And what mindset is that, you may ask? To be a successful dropshipper, you will need to develop the mindset of an entrepreneur. Entrepreneurs run the world because they set out to own it. They do it by cultivating the following attitudes.

Action

The entrepreneurial journey is fraught with numerous problems that often scare people into inactivity. You decide you will first have to work on the best business plan possible. And because you are scared to fail, you hold back, tweaking the business plan for so long that your opportunity passes. Alternatively, there is the research trap in which you decide to learn as much about a subject as possible before starting. Soon enough, you will find information that convinces you that it is a bad idea to even start. So, you give in and start working on the next idea. The action mindset dictates that you just gather the basic information and charge ahead with the plan. You can always perfect later what does not work.

Obsession with cash flow

Cash flow is the lifeblood of business. Without money, you can't make it past a couple of months. Thus, whatever activity you engage in for the sake of the business and every dollar that you put into the business, ask yourself: "How will this help my business bring in money?" If you can't find paying customers, you will end up closing shop sooner or later.

Flexible

You must welcome change and be ready to tweak things and adapt to new situations. If something in your dropshipping business does not work, don't hesitate to change it as long as you maintain the general direction towards your goal. For example, you start off targeting Manga comics fans and a few days of advertising turns out a bigger group of Japanese anime fans, asking if you have this or that product. You don't say, "No, I sell Manga comics and products." Instead, you find a supplier of Japanese anime products and adjust your target market!

Recovery

Successful entrepreneurs are built from a long history of failure. What sets them apart from the rest is that they try every time they fail, adjusting rather than giving up when they fail. If your first dropshipping venture fails, try a different product, a different approach, and soon enough you will be celebrating with the best.

Pro Tip 1: From the word go, plan for the returns your business will bring you and all other issues you will probably face.

Chapter 2: How to Start a Dropshipping Business

Dropshipping is, in essence, the transfer of goods from one party to another through a third party. However, remember that even though you will be doing it online, you will still be bound by the law of the land. When starting a dropshipping business, the things you need to attend to in advance include matters pertaining to the entrepreneurial process like financing and the right product as well as regulatory stuff like licenses, permits, and taxation. In this chapter, we shall look into all these processes in detail.

Finding the Right Product

The only way you will find success in dropshipping is if you sell a product that enough people are willing to pay for. There are three basic strategies for finding the right product: finding trending products, scouring social shopping sites for products, and conducting market research using social networking sites.

The great thing about finding a product that is already trending is that there will always be a market ready for it. You see, with a new product, you always have to start with promotions to inform the market about its existence before making people desire and finally buy it. Trending products are already established as in-demand, so all you have to do is convince enough people to buy from you instead of your competitors. Some of the best places to find trending dropshipping products include Kickstarter, Wish, and Google trends. From the lists featured in these websites, you can identify the products best suited to your store and then work on finding suppliers for them.

Social shopping sites are social networking channels where people share their shopping experiences with others. Pinterest, Wanelo, and Etsy are some of the most popular and most useful websites for identifying products to dropship. Social shopping sites are perfect for that because they feature users who are basically announcing to the world what products they either enjoy using or would like to own. Customer reviews are also featured prominently in these websites. If you want to search for popular products, you can simply look for a category and go through the ratings for the highest rated.

If you can't find products to stock on social shopping or trending sites, you can check out what the market wants by looking through social media yourself. There are numerous forums where people discuss their needs and desires, as well as groups on fitness, gardening, veganism, comic fandom, and other interests on Facebook. Other social networking sites also contain information that can be very handy for an entrepreneur who is looking to establish a dropshipping business with the best product possible.

The rule of picking the products from either of the places discussed above is that it must have a good profit margin. Products below $20 tend to generate little profit, which can make it very hard for your business to gain some traction and make you a profit. Products that sell for more than $150 normally contain a better profit margin and are thus suitable. Basically, the more expensive the product is, the higher the markup you can add on the buying price. However, you have to keep in mind that people are more discerning above the $200 price range. This is to say that while most people won't think twice about buying a $10-$100 product, hardly anyone will make a $200 purchase impulsively. The more costly the product is, the harder you will have to work to bring it to exactly the right market. Failure to do this may result in very poor or no sales at all.

Financing the First Products

With all major online retailers, there is usually a 14- to 21-day lag between making a sale and the time you receive money from your customer. To prevent fraudulent dropshippers from running away with their money and not delivering a product they ordered online, customers also block payments until they actually receive the product. Depending on the supplier and distance between the customer and the delivery center, the delivery may take up to 10 days.

In both of these cases, you will have a willing customer and supplier, but there's no cash at hand to pay the supplier with so that your customer may receive their product. If you don't have the money to pay for a product before the payments remitted by your customer arrives in your account, you will probably end up losing the wholesale. This requires you to find a way to pay your supplier — who will most often demand payments in advance — from your own pocket at first. You can then cover future sales with the money that the customer pays you until there is enough to continue to deduct your cut while still retaining enough money to keep on making purchases with your supplier.

The unpredictable nature of dropshipping often creates situations where you receive few or no orders for a few months, then make thousands of dollars' worth of sales in just a few days. In such instances, you will have to be very imaginative to find a way to fulfill the orders, especially if you don't have enough money to cover the purchase cost. Imagine a situation where you receive orders worth $10,000 in three or four days.

The profit margin on this bulk order you will have to make to your supplier is 15%, so you stand to make $1,500 simply by connecting buyers with suppliers. It also means that you just need $8,500 to fulfill the orders. The only problem is, you don't have that kind of cash.

There are a few options available to you in this kind of a situation. First, you can try to talk with your supplier to use purchase order financing to fulfill the orders. With purchase order financing, you use the customer orders to purchase goods on credit then pay after receiving the money from the customer. The main challenge with this solution is that the supplier in this case also has to deliver, which is an added expenditure. In the event that the price of a commodity is priced inclusive of shipping costs, you can negotiate a simple purchase order financing deal with your supplier, allowing you to fulfill your current orders.

Your second option is to use shopping credit services provided by online payment and financial firms. PayPal gives a particularly helpful product known as PayPal Credit (formerly known as Bill Me Later) that allows users to access credit for purchases over $99 online in revolving credit. These types of products are easy to access and cheap to pay off, considering PayPal credit has no interest rate in the first 6 months.

Realistically, it may take a few months to build your business to a point where you get orders worth $10,000 in a few days.

However, in case it happens immediately (it *could* happen), it is always good to have a backup plan. You can select a supplier that has a flexible financing plan so that you can have the option to negotiate for purchase order financing should you need it. Besides, just because you can start a dropshipping business for less than $200, it does not mean that you should do it without some backup capital. At the very least, ensure that your credit rating is good enough. You never know when you may need it to fulfill a large order.

Licenses and Permits

There are so many things to consider when starting a dropshipping business, such as inventory, e-commerce platform, finance, marketing, branding, and a host of other logistical issues. Moreover, the virtual nature of dropshipping makes it seem like it is an informal venture that requires no licenses and permits to run. Many dropshipping entrepreneurs push off legal formalities completely off their priorities basket and act surprised when the supplier demands for licenses and permits later on.

As far as the government is concerned, an online business is just as real as a traditional retailer. You are making money from a financial activity, so you need to pay taxes. You are participating in the same trading activities, so you will need to apply for the same permits and licenses as a mainstream store. Moreover, if you are serious about it, you should treat your online store like a business entity that can benefit a lot from formal registration with the authorities. So, what documents do you need to start your dropshipping business?

Well, for starters, you are going to need a general business license allowing you to operate a business in your city. Renewable annually or bi-annually, a general license identifies your business as being operational in your jurisdiction for regulation and taxation purposes. You can find the documents required to acquire a business license in the online portal of your local government.

The second document you will need to apply for is a seller's permit. It allows you to collect sales tax on behalf of the government. Because you will probably sell to customers in all 50 states, you need to register so that you can collect from transactions in which you have tax nexus. Previously based on location, nexus laws are changing to accommodate transactions that a retailer does in a state where it does not have a physical footprint. Amz's online sales have created a bit of confusion about who collects state taxes, but it is always better to be prepared in case the duty falls on you in some of your transactions.

The third document you need to operate a dropshipping business is a home occupation permit. When it comes down to it, sometimes the whole "no touching the product" specification of dropshipping falls through. There are dropshipping suppliers on Aliexpress who state that they only ship to buyers with matching order and shipping addresses. This means that you may be forced to receive a product (especially if a supplier is close) and re-ship to the customer. In the event of this happening, you are going to need a home occupation permit, which allows you to ship products from your house. It is not ideal, but it is always better to be prepared for any eventuality.

The fourth thing you will have to do to increase your compliance with rules and regulations is to register your business name. This will help to establish yourself as a legitimate businessperson and your business as a serious entity. Later on in this book, we will discuss the topic of branding. To establish your brand, you must register your business as a sole proprietorship, partnership, or company. If you register your business as a standalone entity, you will also need to apply for an Employer Identification Number from the IRS. This allows you to separate your personal taxation from that of your business.

Pro Tip 2: When choosing your product, go with light and durable over heavy and fragile. The latter is a bit too risky for the rough and tumble of third-party delivery services and might end up broken, which will affect your sales and profits columns.

Chapter 3: The Dropshipping Process

The key players in the supply chain are the manufacturer, wholesaler, and retailer. A product moves along the line before getting to the final consumer who actually uses it. A dropshipper is not featured in the supply chain, because dropshipping is not a role you play. It is a service that a businessperson offers, connecting the manufacturer with the consumer. The services of a dropshipper allow the consumer to cut out other middlemen and buy a product at a considerably lower price than they would otherwise get it.

However, strictly speaking, a dropshipper connects customers with any player in this chain. A manufacturer can put the structures needed in place to ship directly to consumers by enlisting the services of dropshippers, but then so could wholesalers and retailers. It just so happens that manufacturers can offer lower prices on commodities and compete more effectively with retailers and wholesalers. Basically, the fewer the middlemen between you and the manufacturer, the better the pricing you can offer to your customers, the larger the margin you can add, and the more profits you can make from the venture. Running a dropshipping business, you will need to keep this distinction in mind when you go hunting for suppliers. We will cover this in more detail in the coming chapters.

Dropshipping is a four-step process that happens like this:

Phase 1

The customer places their order with a dropshipper. This is done via mobile or PC application or website. After placing the order, the dropshipper and the buyer both receive an automated email confirmation for the order. As soon as the buyer pays for the order, the store software captures it and starts the checkout process, depositing the money in the dropshippers account. Alternatively, if the payment process is expected to take a few days, a confirmation for the beginning of the process.

If you are the dropshipper, make sure that you communicate via PC. The mobile apps do not have the features found in the PC, so using a phone to take orders might lead to you messing up the ordering process. If you desire the mobility of a phone, use a laptop computer, which you can carry around with you to do your work. Your browser must also be the most recent one available. This is critical because Shopify uses the most recent extensions

Phase 2

The second step of the dropshipping process requires the dropshipper to send the order confirmation email to their suppliers. Because the dropshipper registers for a supplier's services with their payment details, the supplier simply charges their credit card with the cost of the product plus shipping and processing fees.

The best suppliers for a Shopify dropshipper are Oberlo Marketplace and AliExpress and beginners often have no problem manually inserting their orders on the suppliers when it is just a few products. However, when you are receiving many orders all at once, it gets a little complicated how you go about fulfilling each one. Before, dropshippers had to manually send each order- a process that required too much time and effort to fulfill massive orders. The smarter thing to do is to automate the process with tools like Around.io, Aftership, Watchlyst, and Beeketing.

Phase 3

The supplier ships the product. With everything in order and the supplier having the product on stock, the supplier is responsible for boxing, transporting, and delivering a product to the customer. The dropshipper supplies the supplier with their logo, address, and other business details upon signing up with them. This allows the supplier to place the drop shipper's logo and return address on the packing slip. The dropshipper is given the tracking number, allowing them to follow up the delivery until it reaches the customer.

When selecting your dropshipping supplier, choose the one who can guarantee the fastest turnaround times. You can take advantage of same-day shipping to advertise your business. This is the process that you have the least control over because everything is left in the hands of the dropshipping supplier. The only thing you can do to increase your confidence in this phase is to vet your suppliers well beforehand and only hire a supplier with a stellar record of order fulfillment.

Phase 4

Notifying the customer of a successful shipment of the product. The dropshipper shares the tracking number with the customer using an inbuilt email interface that is found in most dropshipping stores. The dropshipper pockets the margin between what they paid the supplier to ship the product to the customer, which will be their profit. If by any chance the supplier takes more money to deliver the order that the customer paid for, the dropshipper makes a loss.

And there you go — the dropshipping process in its simplicity. You take an order, send the order to a supplier, confirm that the customer received it, and you are good to go! The only problems arise when the supplier ships the wrong product because they are virtually invisible. The customer only knows the dropshipper, having made their order on his website and receiving a package with their logo and shipping details on it. Any issues will be reported to the dropshipper, not the real seller- the supplier.

To ensure that you stay on top of this whole process, own each and every one of the activities. There is really nothing you don't control because you will choose even the supplier who sends your product but leaves you completely out of the loop. When you find a reliable supplier, hold on tight and don't let go. I cannot emphasize just how important they are to your business. Make your supplier your dropshipping partner and protect your relationship with them. A good supplier (one that does not mess up your order fulfillment process and bring your expensive product returns) is hard to come by. When you find one that you like and they do a good job, stick with them and try to negotiate better terms.

Pro Tip 3: Choose a supplier with a reliable automated dropshipping solution. This advice may not be very applicable in the first days of starting your business, but later, when the orders start really pouring in, you will be glad to have the option to upgrade and use the automatic function.

Chapter 4: How to Start Up the Process In-Depth

The most successful dropshipping businesses are those that follow the start-up process when starting out. In this chapter, we shall look into the startup process for dropshipping business in as much detail as possible.

Finding the Best Suppliers

After finding the niche product to sell to the general market or the niche market to target, you need to find the best supplier to partner with. Finding a supplier is simpler when you have identified the products you would like to sell. Lucky for you, Shopify hosts thousands of suppliers for you to choose from. It also allows you to link your store with Oberlo, with which you can import products from numerous other suppliers from anywhere in the world.

However, as we mentioned before, the reliability of your supplier will play a big part in your success as a dropshipper. Only the best suppliers can guarantee you on-time deliveries and deliver your products intact, helping you avoid the costly returns that plague dropshippers. So, just how do you go about finding the best supplier for your dropshipping business?

First off, understand the distribution channels in your industry. Products made by large manufacturers pass through several middle stages before reaching the final consumer. Manufacturers who produce outside the country often use importers and distributors. Wholesalers often buy in bulk from manufacturers before splitting the product up and selling to retailers. Some manufacturers, especially in the fashion industry, produce directly for their final customers. It is important that you understand exactly where you get your products from in the distribution chain because each of these players has different capacities for special price negotiation, which you will want to do after attaining high volume sales later on.

The second strategy to getting the best supplier for your dropshipping business is to try as much as possible to make the distributor your supplier. Every intermediary between you and the manufacturer adds a little something to the price of the commodity to cover their operations and make some profit. If you can bypass them all and buy straight from the manufacturer at a low price, then your markups can high enough to make it a very worthwhile operation while the price will still be low enough to make you very competitive in the market.

Rather than starting at the Shopify distributor's list for your suppliers, follow the supply chain of every product you have or intend to have on your store and go to the manufacturer. If your current demand does not meet their minimum order requirements, ask them to share with you their list of distributors and contact each one of them, sharing your current demand without exaggerating on the volumes.

The third strategy to finding good suppliers is sifting through major B2B marketplaces. Manufacturers look for markets on these huge marketplaces, including Alibaba, Global Sources, Buyer Zone, and Busy Trade, among others. Oberlo allows you to import products from these wholesale distributors into your Shopify store, swiftly establishing a link between your customers and these multinational distributors.

The fourth strategy is to use online dropshipping groups and forums online to find good distributors. These groups are usually flocked by dropshippers who are looking to help each other. You can post questions and receive insightful feedback right there. Another place to interact with fellow dropshippers is in trade shows. Here, you can meet up with fellow professionals and discuss partnerships. For example, if you need a product from a particular distributor, but your demand does not meet their minimum order requirements, you can meet people with similar problems in trade shows and join hands with them, pool your demand together, and meet the threshold for cheaper products from the manufacturer or distributor.

Uploading Products Onto Your Shopify Store

Every product you upload to your store requires a product name, description, and brand. Once you have discussed all the pertinent issues with your supplier, you will have to start manually uploading the .CSV sheets of their products onto your store. The .CSV files act as a means of linking the supplier's products with your own account, automatically reflecting things like the number of products in stock among other functions.

Before starting to upload your products on your Shopify store, first download the .CSV files onto your computer. To edit the product, you open the .CSV file in Excel or Google Sheets. This allows you to change price, pictures, description, and any other details you might want to customize.

You then open your Shopify website and click on the **Admin** tab. When this opens, click on **Products**> **All Products**> **Import**>**Import products by .CSV file**>**Choose File.** The platform automatically leads you to the files in your computer and you upload them onto your store.

Whenever you want to update existing products (making changes to the listed price, inserting new pictures, etc.), you just edit the original .CSV file on your spreadsheet program then start the uploading process, selecting **Replace any current products that have the same handle** on the **Import** tab.

How to Set Up a Payment System

As a dropshipper, you will be selling to customers from all over the world. Whatever means of payment you choose to use for your website, you will want it to be easy to use, accessible, and available in as many countries as possible. A customer may choose not to buy from your store simply because you don't have the means of payment they use when shopping online. For many, the hassle of starting the verification process of a new payment method is just too much. They would much rather find a dropshipper who accepts their preferred payment method.

Therefore, part of the research you should do while identifying a niche market is to determine the payment method most of them use. Ideally, your store should facilitate payments by every customer's preferred payment system. Therefore, you should have the most dominant payment system in the country you are selling to or as many systems as possible to ensure that not a single customer will ever be locked out of your store because they don't have the payment system by which you make money. Luckily, there are payment means that are fast, secure, and readily available online. By order of their availability around the world, they include PayPal, 2checkout, Skrill, Authorize, and Stripe.

Paypal guarantees you coverage to any country in the world and is the most recommended payment system. Not only is it easy to set up, but it is also more secure, easily convertible, and it provides PayPal Credit, a service that allows you to overdraw your account if you need more money to cover an order. PayPal also supports all major credit cards like Citibank, Visa, American Express, and Mastercard. When opening an account with PayPal, be sure to open a business one. The tools available in the business account will come in handy in the tracking of your sales. Once you open an account, you simply select the PayPal widget on Shopify, link it to your account, and you are all set to receive payments.

2checkout is available in about 87 of all countries in the world, including most of the thirsty world. It also supports most of the credit cards PayPal does. It works well when combined with PayPal because it grants you access to the largest portion of the online-playing populace.

Stripe is another payment gateway based in America that supports major credit cards. However, its popularity is mostly limited to the Commonwealth countries of America, Canada, and Australia.

Skrill is another excellent payment system with a fully integrated online payment system. With a 1.9% checkout fee, Skrill is considerably less costly as a payment system. Its main shortcoming is the low penetration levels.

Finally, we have Authorize.net. Available in 33 countries and supporting many of the major credit card issuers, this payment system is somewhat limited but still quite useful. It is especially preferred by older generations as one of the older online gateways for credit card payments. If your target market features older people, you should definitely check out Authorize.net.

With each of these payment systems, you can download extensions for free to put in your website. These extensions link your customers with your own preferred payment reception method, allowing them to buy from your preferred supplier through your store.

Customer Service

Here is the thing about customer service for your dropshipping business. If you don't provide it, no one else will. Suppliers are often too busy fulfilling orders for thousands of other businesses to focus on every one of your customers. It should be your prerogative to put in place the systems to track orders and communicate with customers when anything goes wrong. Luckily, customer service really boils down to effective communication. If your supplier fails to deliver a product to your customer. The customer will call you to complain and probably leave an unfavorable review on your website. However, if you call and inform them that an unavoidable hitch has affected your delivery systems and the order will be x late, they will appreciate your forthrightness and be more forgiving.

Pro Tip 4: Part of vetting your suppliers should include getting a sample product from them. This allows you to take better pictures, write winning product descriptions, and even create a video demonstrating its use. Remember that the dropshipping field is very crowded and anything that gives you an advantage over the competition is a very welcome opportunity.

Chapter 5: Niches and Products

The 80/20 rule states that a business makes 80% of its profits from 20% of its customers. These are the people who buy in volumes, make repeat purchases, and spread the business name through word of mouth. This is exactly why identifying a niche market is so important. You find the portion of the market that is best suited to be a target for your business. Marketing and selling to them become more easily because they have an actual need that your product fulfills.

Identifying a Niche

Niche products are those that fascinate a small section of the population. They include fashion products (with their numerous sub-niches), organic food products, pet supplies, electronic goods, baby clothes, etc. With a niche product, you narrow down on a certain section of the market and focus on them only. It helps you to focus all your efforts on that particular demographic rather than marketing for everyone, as in mass marketing. Manufacturers in niche markets are usually small and highly specialized, with some actually producing their products by hand. Handmade is actually a niche within the fashion category. It speaks of luxury and uniqueness and attracts higher prices.

Identifying and ascertaining the viability of a niche is hands down the most important processes a dropshipper goes through before starting up. It can also be incredibly stressful because it is often the difference between success and failure later on. You should never rely exclusively on e-commerce experts and the online courses they peddle to find your niche. They will just give you a list of products and tell you that they are niche, but they will do the same with thousands of other dropshipping entrepreneurs, defeating the very definition of a niche by making them available to numerous dropshippers.

A niche market is a specific sector of the buying population that is not being reached by a product. Niche markets are usually neglected by mainstream businesses and you can reap huge rewards by tailoring your company to serve their needs. To find niche markets, just look at the areas and sections of the market served by the biggest businesses in your area then try to find the places where their marketing and sales networks do not reach. It can be a sector that no one has ever thought to look into or a certain utility of a product that people ignore. By unlocking these sections of the market, you can create a niche for yourself very easily.

An example of a niche market is that if you look at the pet supplies market and realize that there are no supplies for comfort pet owners in the Delaware Valley region, you can start your dropshipping business by focusing specifically on this market.

When going niche, you have to ensure as much as possible that you are entering a field with few players. However, it must be promising enough that you will still make money off it. It is always a balance between uniqueness and potential for profit-making. You must look for markets that are large enough so that it is a sustainable balance that must be achieved if your niche is to prove profitable, otherwise, it won't be sustainable enough over the long term.

The first process of identifying a trend is brainstorming. Here, you simply observe the dropshipping community and try to come up with gaps in the products offered and markets served. This process requires a purely intellectual brute force. Once you have brainstormed a list of likely products, you start the real research using Google Trends, Facebook, Trend Hunter, Instagram, Aliexpress.

Google Trends

To narrow down your search for the perfect niche product, start with a Google search. You may be surprised to find a great one on the search results. However, when all you find is what everyone else is selling (the perfect recipe for dangerous price wars), then it is time to go deeper.

Google Trends is an analytics tool that allows you to evaluate a given item in all Google databases stored by the company since 2004. Considering Google is currently the undisputed champion of online searches, this is a large database to dive into. You can use it to gauge the popularity of a brainstormed product by looking at the search trends in the past few months or years. You can compare the popularity of different products to see how it performs against the competition. By modifying the search results to receive data from specific areas, you can identify niche markets as well.

Facebook

People interact freely on Facebook. There are numerous groups dedicated to various interests, including television shows, gaming, pets, dating, etc. After brainstorming a particular product you can dropship, you can join Facebook forums dedicated to that field and ask something like, "Anyone know where I can buy a customized kitty shirt?" If there is already a big group of businesses offering the same product, then it is time to go back to the drawing board and try again. Products with dormant groups or where interaction and enthusiasm are low are probably not in that much demand to support your business.

Trend Hunter

Trend Hunter uses big data to provide business people like you with reliable and current market intelligence. The website conducts detailed market research and makes recommendations on product ideas based on consumer interest and purchase patterns. You can take advantage of these listings to find your own product by comparing the trending products listed on the website with those featured on Amz, Shopify, and other dropshipping sites. This way, you will probably identify trends before the rest of the dropshipping community finds out about them and floods the market with them and profit from first mover's benefits.

Instagram

Instagram is another social networking site that can present you with a great many ideas for niche products. People are always posting their lives on Instagram, often under a bunch of hashtags, for the whole world to see. You can insert the keywords of the products you have brainstormed and see what kind of results turn up. If many people are expressing their desire to own something, then there is an unfulfilled market out there. The good thing about Instagram is that you can later use it to reach the very people who helped you identify a niche product and sell it to them.

Dropshipping sites

Before making your own listing, it is advisable to take a trip around the dropshipping stores like Shopify, to identify products that are in massive demand and those that have few merchants selling them. Amz is especially insightful, being by far the largest e-commerce website and with its front pages filled with products in different categories.

Evergreen Niche Products

When selecting a niche product, is also advisable to find one that you can continue selling for a while. These are the lifestyle products that people are always spending money on. For example, movie fans are always looking for collectibles. Same with comic fans. Even though the printed comic books are being replaced by electronic ones and movies fast, the old collectibles (e.g., toys, printed shirts, and other merchandise) are still in high demand.

Listed in order of their lucrativeness, the following five niches are worth looking into.

Sports and hobbies

As the fitness craze continues to sweep through the country, home gym supplies are only going to become more popular online. The same goes for weight loss products.

Gaming

Gaming fans will always be looking for products to game on and to celebrate their hobby. The PC Gaming market is worth over $30 billion. If you can capitalize on this, your store would be set for life.

Beauty

This is one of the most popular e-commerce markets. Every year, dropshippers sell billions' worth of make-up and decorative products all over the world. And as the population grows and more people start buying online, the market is only going to expand.

Fashion

Fashion products are popular not just among humans but also for pets and events like Halloween.

Home security

This is an emerging niche that has massive potential. There are numerous sub-niches in this market and new products are always being launched, invigorating the market.

Exploiting a Niche

What you do while identifying a niche is that you build trust. When you identify a very specific product or market and focus all your efforts on it, you can easily learn everything there is to know about it and establish yourself as an authority. You then build trust among the customers who identify you as an authority on the product category of your choice. To look at this from the customer's perspective, pretty much anyone would rather buy a camping stove from someone who focuses either on different heating supplies or on camping gear. Make yourself the person everyone in a particular category would rather go to than your competitors and you will have yourself a winning store.

To build trust and set yourself as the leader, you must engage your target market on every available social networking site. You need to Tweet, Instagram, post on Facebook, create Pinterest boards, and YouTube videos about your selected niche product/market. By saturating every social media with posts about you and your product, everyone will come to identify you as the real authority in that sector! This will be discussed further on branding, but imagine if someone went to search for video-making equipment and found videos of you demonstrating how to set up parabolic shots on YouTube, Facebook posts inviting people to a seminar on YouTube vlogging, and Twitter updates of the seminar. On your website, they find articles touching on different areas of the video shooting process. These are the kind of practices niche dropshippers employ.

Pro Tip 5: A niche that serves a passionate market is the best one you can ever find. People are more compelled to take advantage of offers for passion products like yoga mats, training shoes, camping supplies, or mountain-climbing gear much more than common products like furniture. People buy more of the things they enjoy using, so give them more of that.

Chapter 6: Taking Care of Supplier Relations

Your relationship with suppliers will turn out to be the most valuable asset your dropshipping business will ever have. They are your most valuable partners as you navigate the rough and tumble of dropshipping. If you are to survive the competition from your fellow dropshippers, you must maintain the best relationship with them.

Supplier Support

It is impossible to run a dropshipping business without the support of your suppliers. Because they do most of the work, it is accurate to say that suppliers are the most essential players in the dropshipping process. The advantages of having a dependable supplier include getting good, quality items, receiving better support, and having peace of mind.

Quality items

Put yourself in the shoes of your customers. Have you ever ordered an item online that you were so excited about only to receive and be underwhelmed? Well, so has everyone else!

Sometimes, a dropshipper overstates the quality of their product to entice buyers. Other times, the supplier simply dumps their worst products on customers from their least-favorite or newbie dropshippers. The result is that they get unsatisfied customers, bad reviews, poor sales, losses — you name it. You see, even though the dropshipper/supplier relationship is a business one, there is the human element of it. Behind the basic website, email address, and landline telephone lies a human being. And this human being will be inclined, just like every other person, to treat their friends better. Instead of complaining about how unfair that is, just befriend your supplier — even in the strictly business sense of that word. You won't regret it.

Better support

Just as I mentioned above, suppliers will pay closer attention to the requirements of their strategic partners than the orders of everyone else. Even among official business partners, establishing a strong foundation based on mutual support and trust is critical for success. Your supplier will be your unofficial business partners in your dropshipping venture. Communicate better with them. Take the time to inform them of your plans for the future and collaborations you can have together to make the process more effective. If you respect their business and their role in yours, they will reciprocate in kind and possibly elevate your business to great new heights.

Peace of mind

In dropshipping, anything can go wrong at any time. You will feel the loss of control because you cannot handle more than half of the fulfillment processes of your own business. Knowing that a trusted partner is taking care of your business will give you the peace of mind you need to carry out other functions to keep yourself profitable.

Building a Good Supplier Relationship

There is a very specific recipe for forming a great relationship with your suppliers, but it requires you to put in some extra work into your day-to-day operations.

1. Be friendly

As mentioned above, behind the computer on the other side is usually a person. Being friendly with them will go a long way in helping you maintain a good relationship.

2. Pay promptly

Your supplier requires the money you give him so that they can keep the business operational. Paying your bills consistently within the given timeframe will set you apart as a reliable partner who understands the business process. This is especially critical when the supplier has extended you a line of credit.

3. Check in

It may seem like a bit of an overkill, but take the time to reach out to the supplier to simply chat about business. You can exchange intel about which products are selling better than others, voice any concerns (if any) about their delivery services, and discuss new products. You might be surprised to find your business doing very well because your supplier recommended a certain product.

4. Be reliable

As much as you need the supplier to fulfill your customers' needs in time and with the best of their products, you must also be reliable to them. All emails and calls must be answered promptly and for calls, any missed ones must be returned as soon as possible. Any purchases you negotiate must be followed through. A last minute change of mind will only estrange your supplier.

5. Be sensible

Just because you have a great relationship with your supplier does not mean that you should exploit them with last minute orders. This creates too much stress for the supplier and could lead to undue friction.

6. Address issues promptly

Any time there is an issue with the product your supplier delivered for a customer, talk to them first and let them defend their actions. Sometimes, reaching out to talk about an issue might be just the thing your supplier needs to fix its business and increase its profitability in the long run. If they are good (and they should be), then they will appreciate your feedback as a great learning opportunity.

7. Share insights

What you give is what you may get. This particular strategy is rather selfish, but it establishes a semblance of quid-pro-quo, which means that the supplier feels compelled to return the favor with one of their own. This can be a great way to motivate your suppliers to share with you ideas about new products that you can start selling.

Managing Multiple Suppliers

A single supplier is easy to deal with. The relationship is monogamous, which makes it easier for you to focus on both your needs. However, as you build up your store, you will realize that you need more than one supplier to serve your ever-expanding customer base. Even if you are operating such a niche business that one supplier can fulfill all your needs, putting all your eggs in one basket is quite risky. Stuff happens, and the next thing you know, you are back to square one trying to find a new supplier for your business. If you are more interested in streamlining the business than establishing a huge dropshipping brand, sticking with one supplier might not be such a bad thing. For the ambitious dropshipper with dreams of owning a large dropshipping operation, you will want to find suppliers that overlap so that your business can function even when one of them goes out of stock or is unable to deliver to your customers for one reason or another.

The multiple supplier route may be quite attractive, especially when your store is doing really well. Every supplier will want to be on your good side with timely deliveries and the best price offers. Your business could do with suppliers outdoing each other to offer you the best deal in the hope of enticing you to source exclusively from them.

On the other hand, consider that for every supplier relationship you form, you will have to build and maintain a strong relationship using the seven-point formula outlined above. If you are running your store alone, the effort may become too much.

All in all, multiple suppliers are a common feature in the dropshipping business. For sure, they require greater effort on your part to maintain the relationship, but it is not all that bad.

With some extra tools, you can even turn your multiple suppliers into your store's best selling point.

Managing inventory

With multiple suppliers, you may not be in a position to coordinate via phone or email about inventory levels. Instead, you can approach the supplier and have them sync their inventory with your store through third-party applications. You can then follow the progress of your orders from the warehouse to the customer's doorstep right along with the suppliers. This will give you much-needed clarity on pending and fulfilled orders. This enables you to give your customers very confident and informed updates on the status of their order any time they ask for it.

Another advantage of synced inventory is that it hides a product from your store when a supplier runs out. This helps you avoid those awkward moments when you have to turn a customer away because a product that is listed on your store is not in stock in a supplier's warehouses.

Managing deliveries

You don't get multiple suppliers unless your store is really huge and you have determined that a single supplier can't fulfill all your orders. When you have a few suppliers making deliveries at the same time, following all your orders can get very complicated. Let's say a customer ordered six different products: 2 stocked by A Suppliers, 1 supplied by B Suppliers, and 3 by C Suppliers and Logistics. You need to make sure that all six arrive at the same time; otherwise, the customer will be confused and suspicious of your delivery system.

To take care of these kinds of scenarios, it is always advisable to hire a third-party logistics company to take care of special orders. You will then negotiate for special prices with your suppliers for the products you deliver out of your own pocket.

Conflict Resolution

In the course of running your business, conflicts will emerge not just with customers, but also with suppliers, payment provider, and peripheral service providers. Conflict is often necessary to strengthen a relationship. It shows that people know exactly what they want and are willing to fight for it. However, too much of it might sour things up. Resolving conflicts is a very important part of running a business. You simply must learn how to do it in a healthy manner. The process includes accommodating, collaborating, and compromising.

When you are wrong and the other party has grown frustrated with your antics leading to conflict, accommodation is the way to go. Here, you recognize that you are wrong and graciously agree to take the blame, promising to be more careful about repeating the same mistake again. For example, you have been less attentive to payments and a fraudulent credit card has been used to make a purchase on your platform. When your payment services provider confronts you with the accusation of laxity, you don't justify your actions. You own them and promise to do better in the future.

Collaborating is a strategy in which two parties resolve to work together to get to the bottom of an issue that is creating conflict. In this setup, you work together with your supplier, service provider, or payment provider to ensure that an issue never repeats again even if it is not your fault that it happened. You may not be particularly happy with the outcome, but you resolve the conflict and continue to work together. For example, a breakdown in the supplier's communication chain leads to them shipping the wrong product to the right customer or vice versa. Instead of getting infuriated, you recognize that breakdowns happen to anyone and work with them to ensure that their communication channels are upgraded to a more reliable level so that a situation like that never happens again.

Finally, there is the idea of compromise, which is similar to collaborating. The only difference is that, in this case, both members of the conflict played a part in its formation. Using the example above, if you sent the wrong product codes and the supplier failed to verify them while sending the tracking number, then both of you played a part in the conflict. The compromise can be to split the difference of any costs incurred in the whole blunder. Even if it will leave you both unhappy, you will have gotten your fair blame and cost for your part in it.

Pro Tip 6: A shipping partner comes in very handy when handling complicated orders when your market share grows and you start dealing with multiple suppliers. Signing up with a third-party logistics company like ShipBob will give you access to some very good deals and take care of those orders that a single supplier simply can't fulfill.

Chapter 7: Sales Channels

As a dropshipper, there are a few sales channels open for you to sell your products. The reality is that Shopify is not recognized as one of the major e-commerce websites where people flock to buy online. This honor is enjoyed by Amz and in America and a few other e-commerce websites including Alibaba internationally. To increase the reach of your business, you will have to diversify and establish selling counters for your business on these sites as well. What's great is that Shopify is totally okay with this arrangement. It gives its users the tools they need to link their accounts with these major e-commerce websites. This means that even with Shopify as your home and operating base, you can still take advantage of other dropshipping sales channels. In this chapter, we shall look at these sales channels, the pros and cons of each, and how to incorporate each one into your sales strategy for your dropshipping business.

Shopify

Even though it is better suited to hosting merchants than for selling, Shopify is still considered a legit selling channel because it enables you to sell on the platform to buyers attracted from your social media and other marketing efforts. With Shopify, the concept you bring to bear is deep linking whereby they come from Facebook, Pinterest, the Shopify links you advertise with, and other creative ideas you may come up with. This topic will be discussed in full in the following chapter.

Pro Tip 7: Always use alternative dropshipping platforms as sales channels. Other than the two discussed in this chapter, look into AliExpress, SaleHo, Doba, and others.

Chapter 8: Optimizing Your Website for Selling

This chapter is basically about attracting buyers to your Shopify store. There are certain things that go a long way in attracting shoppers to your store, albeit small. These include the name, graphic design of your website, and product arrangement. It works much like traditional stores. A good name gives you the opportunity to set yourself apart, generates content for marketing and advertisements, and forms the basis for the formulation of a brand identity. In this chapter, we will look into these things and describe how you can totally crush the process of setting up your store by observing the pointers therein.

Choosing a Name

A strong brand name is a huge advantage over the competition. The name you give to your store will form the basis for the brand you will start to establish as soon as you sign up for that particular domain on Shopify. However, be very careful while selecting a name for your business. Your customers will differentiate and judge your store based on the name you give it.

Have you ever been shopping online and, unable to decide between a variety of products or businesses to shop from, simply went with the one that had the catchiest, most trustworthy-sounding name? Well, so has everyone else! Our brains make associations with familiar objects, whether it be in the decision on what product to buy, restaurant to patronize, or movie to watch. If it does not sound right, then it probably won't be a good fit; that is the default setting of most of us. As a business person, you can learn to take advantage of this reality to attract customers.

You see, even though you can't possibly predict the name that everyone would most easily relate to, you can use your own intuition and a bit of research to get a pretty good idea. Test your business name idea with a few friends and take their opinions. If they think your business name sounds great, then you can proceed to name your Shopify domain. If the people closest to you think your store sounds anything but great, you may consider going back to the drawing board. The following tips will guide you in choosing a name that most buyers will identify with.

Keep it simple and short

Short names are easier to pronounce, write, and remember. So, your name should sound good and elicit nice memories so that people remember it. Even though we don't say them out aloud, we remember names by thinking about the sound they make. A short name also fits snugly into the header of your store's landing page. If you must go with more than one word, select words that have similar or complementary sounds like Anime Maxime or Total Rip Fitness. If you find yourself stuck on the name, you can consider asking the graphics designer who designs your logo to start by suggesting a few names.

Be unique

Before naming your store, spy on all the other dropshippers in the same category. These will be your direct competitors and knowing their names will help you to avoid choosing the most obvious name for the category. You can identify it by counting the density of certain keywords in all your competitor's names. After checking all the names out, brainstorm the most unique name a company in your category could have and still remain relevant. A word of advice: don't be hasty when selecting a name for your business. It is okay to take a few days until you find the perfect match.

Be creative

Try to imagine what a person feels when they hear the name of your product. What kind of memories or sensations does it arouse? This is the direction to take when naming your business. Think of what you will be selling and try to invoke whatever sensations it arouses in your buyers. This way, customers will always click on your store whenever they conduct a search for a product featured in your store because your name triggered certain sections of their minds and pricked their curiosity.

The Store Design

A poorly designed website may not just lead to poor conversion rates. Instead, it can actively chase potential customers out of your store! Studies have shown up to 20% of online shoppers have made the decision not to buy from a store because the design was bad and the interface was no user optimized. The common reasoning behind this phenomenon is that customers think, "If you cannot take the time to design a proper website, how can I trust you to deliver my product?" When the online store is the only place your customers will view the product they are about to commit their money to buy, the stakes for great design and easy navigation go even higher.

On Shopify (and pretty much every other sales channel), you compete with professional dropshippers. We are talking about people who have to spend up to ten years dropshipping, learning new tricks, and figuring out ways to give themselves an advantage over newbies like you. To compete with the dropshipping wizards, you will have to present your customers with the best shopping experience of their lives. A website that looks good makes the seller look more credible. These are decisions customers make as they open your merchant's account. If they like what they see, they might continue to view the products and possibly buy something. When the website looks unprofessional and uninspired, potential customers hit the back button and look for the next best thing.

Shopify features hundreds of themed store designs for its users, creating the perfect hassle-free design process and giving all users — even those with no design experience whatsoever — the opportunity to put together a good selling platform. Even though themes are nearly uniform and based on a simple template, they have that quasi-professional look that is just good enough to trick visitors into believing that your website was done by a professional. If you want yours to stand out more, you can always hire a web designer to do the work for you. Alternatively, you can just mess around with the design yourself until it is right. Either way, check out websites like allbirds.com, pipsnacks.com, leifshop.com, and bearbrand.com.

They all have very simplistic websites that speak of sophistication and quality brands. That would not be a very idea for you to copy.

Finally, do not forget to optimize your website for mobile. More and more people are using their mobile phones to shop online. If you design your shop for desktop without creating a version for the mobile phone, you are missing out on a great opportunity to make money.

Optimizing the Product Page

Traditional stores use visual merchandising to help customers to locate the products they want more easily. It also allows managers to come up with the optimal layout for the store. One of the proven strategies of visual merchandising is placing the most commonly purchased products closest to the entrance and items that are usually bought together close together. They help supermarkets increase sales volumes and thus profitability. You can do the same with your online store.

Your product page provides the customer with the information they need to make a decision about purchasing a product. It streamlines the decision-making process and builds the customer's confidence in your store enough that they actually buy. A product page comprises of four different components:

user experience, brand, copywriting, and product placement. When executed properly, all these components work together to generate very good conversion rates for a dropshipping website. The following ideas work great to bring your product page to the levels of conversion you need:

A clear call to action

The whole idea behind bringing the customer to your store is to get them to buy. The **Add to Cart** button is the most important part of the page in this regard. It invites the customer to make the commitment to buy. Ensure that you make it simple and to the point, with no distractions or clatter.

Good product image

The biggest challenge in e-commerce is that your customer does not touch, taste, or see the products before buying them. The only thing that a customer sees is the product photo. As you'd expect, customers judge a product by how well its photo has been captured. A great product image generates greater confidence and higher conversion rates, with a poor image having the inverse effect.

Product description

The product description adds to the reality created by the image to give your potential customers a better impression of the product. Descriptions of colors, scents, and other features make a product more realistic. It also increases the desire of a customer to own a product. It is easy to fall for long jumbled paragraphs when creating a product description. It is just as easy to fall back on bullets methodically listing the selling points of your product. However, it is more effective to infuse the product description with your brand image, creating a relatable persona that your customers can identify with.

Featured Customers

Customers on the internet are usually looking for any kind of proof that you are as good as your word. Social proof is the best tool for confidence building because it lets them know that they are not the only people to have given your products a try. Glowing reviews from previous customers at the bottom of your landing page will give visitors the confidence they need to go through with the purchase.

Testimonials are especially effective in making customers believe in you as a seller when you are not a strong brand.

Ideally, the featured customers should be satisfied with your service delivery enough for them to leave the glowing review you then highlight for new visitors. You can also give yourself a leg over by requesting a customer to rate you and leave a comment. If you get an institutional buyer, they will appreciate the extra publicity featuring on your testimonials page will bring to them. If customers are not very eager to leave glowing reviews, you can entice them with a small discount. As long as your store lives up to the hype, there should be no problem there.

Affiliate Marketing

Another very effective way to get customers to buy on your website is to get into affiliate partnerships with other dropshippers and refer customers to each other. Affiliates pay each other a small share of the profits they make from a sale in commission. When you get customers from an affiliated seller, your sales volumes will increase and your store will become more profitable. When you refer buyers to affiliates, you will earn money without actually dealing with the hectic sales execution process of order routing, follow-up, and payment processing.

There are numerous affiliate marketing programs on Shopify. After setting up your store and optimizing it for selling, you should consider signing up for one. You can then choose the offers you promote on your pages, post them, and watch as the money flows. When posting your own affiliate offer, ensure that it is worthwhile for the dropshipper who will pick it. The commission fee is high enough to enable them to dedicate time and effort to promote your products.

To make affiliate marketing a revenue source, you will have to create a blog, vlog, or become very active on social media. Through these channels, you will promote your own business and make your store profitable. You can then suggest sellers of commodities you don't have on your store to your followers. They buy where you tell them to buy because they trust you. This brings us to the golden rule of affiliate marketing; do not recommend a product you are not 100% confident about. If you wouldn't use it, don't promote it. The last thing you want is for your followers to blame you for misleading them into buying a disappointing product.

Pro Tip 8: Your success as a dropshipper is hinged on the way you present your products on your store, among other things. It may be hard, but it is always worthwhile to create the perfect product description, use the right image, and create a great user experience.

Chapter 9: How to Manage Inventory

Inventory in dropshipping is used loosely because a dropshipper never maintains physical products. Instead, the suppliers who fulfill customer orders placed on your store manages all your inventory for you. This is not to say that you don't play a part in this very important process. It is the job of the dropshipper to ensure that all the products listed on their store are available in the supplier's warehouse. Managing inventory in a dropshipping business entails synchronizing your store to the supplier's warehouse, dealing with returned products, and "out of stock." In chapter 6, we discussed maintaining a good relationship with a supplier and synching your store to their warehouses. In this chapter, we shall look into the issue of product returns and fraudulent payments.

Product Returns and Customer Service

As unexciting as it is, a return policy is necessary for every dropshipping business. It is required by law and, by every dropshipping marketplace, acting as a guarantee that your customer will not be left in the dark should the product not meet their expectations. It does not just allow customers who are displeased with the product your supplier shipped them to return it and possibly get a new one; it builds confidence and makes them more likely to buy from you again.

A generous return policy means that customers can count on you to refund their money or replace the product if it is not up to par with their expectations. This is especially important because customers usually don't see the product until it arrives at their doorstep. On the other hand, you have to ensure that the return policy is not too generous as to encourage willy nilly returns.

You have to design a return policy that protects you and your customer, giving you both some semblance of reprieve from dissatisfaction and exploitation. Instead of looking at it as an inconvenience that takes your food out of your mouth just as you are about to chew on it, look at it as a way to build trust and confidence with the people who will support your business days to come.

The great thing about going about designing a return policy is that it forces you to answer one very simple question. "How confident are you about your business process?" Depending on your level of certainty, your return policy will either be daring, balanced, or self-protectionist. Basically, your returns policy becomes your product guarantee and customers are more assured and likely to trust businesses with a daring guarantee.

The more confident the guarantee is, the more trustworthy it will be, and the more customers it will reassure and appeal to.

To come up with a return policy that covers both you and the customer, observe the following rules.

1. A return policy should cover all the bases. If you are selling a durable product, the customer wants to know that it will last them for a long time. It is a priority. Thus, you can place it very prominently on the website to act as part of your marketing.

2. If you don't want to use returns as part of your marketing, then at least make it easy for visitors to find it. Accessibility is paramount, especially when you start out as an untested business.

3. A customer who checks your return policy has probably already made the decision to buy and is just nervous about your ability to deliver exactly what they want. Be friendly and reassuring rather than standoffish. Some return policies read like a carefully drafted document releasing the seller from any obligation to the buyer. A simple message like this will do: "If your product does not meet your expectations, [Store Name] accepts returns on orders up to 30 days after delivery. Kindly send an email to returns@storename.com and we will take care of the rest."

4. In your communications with a dissatisfied customer, be clear about who takes care of what. Customers are happier

when the seller meets shipping costs and you will minimize your loss if you replace rather than repay for the product. Never take the business out of returns.

5. If you make a mistake and send a customer the wrong product, you inconvenience them greatly. Even if you have a busy shop and are dealing with thousands of orders, don't make it sound like you are avoiding taking the fall. Own the mistake, make up for it, and hope that the customer likes your way of doing business enough to come back again. If you are hard on yourself about those mistakes you have made that have resulted in a return, you will be more careful about making them in the future.

How to Deal With "Out of Stock"

Someday, when you are busy kicking ass and filling orders, raking in dollars by the spadefuls, your supplier will just run out of the product that your customers (and you) are most excited about. Now, you may think that running out is just a temporary glitch and your supplier will restock and soon enough you will get back to selling. And this might even be the case: the situation may not last for more than just a few hours. However, a few hours is all the time it takes for you to lose the momentum you have worked months to build. When you are starting out, you simply cannot afford to have any glitches whatsoever.

Any time a customer attempts to buy from your store and cannot, you lose more than just the profit you would have made on the purchase. First off, this customer will probably go to your competitor's store and make a purchase. So, your competitor wins. Secondly, they will trust the store where they managed to find something they really wanted, so you lose some momentum in creating a loyal customer base. You simply cannot allow this to happen.

There are two ways to deal with the issue of products going out of stock. The first one is to have a backup supplier and use them interchangeably. The chances that a product will go out of stock in your two suppliers' warehouses are very slim. You can ensure uninterrupted sales on your store this way and effectively secure your business against losses. The underside of this strategy is that you will have to juggle two supplier relationships to cover all your products. If you are supplied by more than one supplier for the products you sell on your store, this can get very stressful.

The alternative is to simply hide the out of stock product from your products page. Visitors will not know that you are out of stock because they won't see any out of stock products. For those repeat customers who already know and count on you to deliver a certain product for them, they will probably contact you to demand an explanation. You can then explain the situation to them and promise to fulfill their orders as soon as possible.

Nevertheless, there is another reason why taking an out of stock product from your product page can be such a good idea. Sitting there but unable to generate any cash flow, an out-of-stock product is exactly like an empty shelf in a supermarket. You should treat it the same way store managers treat it- replace it with something that you can actually sell and make money.

Dealing With Fraud

As lucrative as it is, dropshipping carries with it some very serious problems of credit card fraud. Credit card fraud is rampant on e-commerce sites — if you are not careful enough, you may fall victim, too. The two most common problems related to credit card crime include fraudulent orders and stolen or false credit cards used to make a purchase in your store. In both cases, banks usually automatically deduct the amount you were paid from your account and refund it to the (usually complaining) credit card holder.

A fraudulent purchase is pretty unfair because it is the merchant who pays for the order, including the forward and return shipping fees. Even worse, dropshippers suspend or close entirely merchant accounts that have suffered a certain number of chargebacks. This inconveniences your store and forces you to go through a long and unnecessary verification process before you can be allowed back in. Therefore, you must learn to identify the signals of a fraudulent transaction. They include:

Differing billing and shipping addresses

During Christmas, a person buying a product and shipping it to a relative in a different state is simply a part of the holiday cheer. At any other time, different billing and shipping address is worth noting. The same goes for differing names on the shipping and billing addresses.

Suspicious email addresses

Gmail, Outlook, Yahoo!, and iCloud mail are all free-service email servers available for free to the public. People who use their work emails to buy online will have a customized server. Those intending to cause mischief, on the other hand, often use private servers that allow them to open accounts without using their legitimate personal data. Bookmark any email you receive that looks suspicious and try to establish a line of communication with the user behind it. It is better to do this than risk serving a fraudster and having to suffer the consequences.

Rush shipment request on a huge purchase

It is easier to fall for this one because your business mind goes automatically into the beautiful profit you stand to make when the transaction is complete. Imagine receiving an order worth $50,000 that the customer wants to be shipped ASAP. You will probably start calculating your margin, scheming up ways to convince the supplier to give you a better price for the large volume purchase.

Credit criminals employ the "slip under the cracks" technique whereby they place orders at odd hours. The dropshipper, looking to impress them with quick turnaround time, fulfills the order without vetting the customer. If you are making a margin of 16%, you stand to make $8,000 with a $50,000 order. But just imagine what would happen if it turned out to be a false order. You end up shouldering a fraudulent credit card transaction of up to $50,000.

Rerouting packages

Orders that have been purchased with a stolen credit card may be shipped out using the original delivery address, but midway through the fraudster calls and changes the address, bypassing the internal security measures used to identify possible fraudulent orders.

Alternatively, you can use a third-party fraud prevention service to screen payments on your website. These include ClearSale, a fraud analysis firm that uses AI to identify threats more accurately than a suspicious human mind ever could.

Pro Tip 10: If you want to start a serious dropshipping operation that is free from massive risk, you should consider insuring yourself against fraud, either with paid fraud detection tools or a payment insurer. Not only are these tools more reliable, but they also free you up from the constant worry of fraudulent payments.

Chapter 10: How to Destroy the Competition

Winning in the dropshipping game is one part running a good business and two parts beating the competition. Every customer who buys in another dropshipper's store is a customer (and revenue) you forfeit. The less of this revenue you forfeit, the better it will be for your store. In this chapter, we look at the strategies you can use to beat the competition, including the proven winner; spying on them.

Spying on the Competition

A competitive field makes it harder for you to get new customers, make new sales, and expand your business. However, it also allows you a better business person because it forces you to think about things like market share. In any highly competitive field, competitors are always trying to knock each other off the playing ground. You have to be strong, tough, and innovative to figure out ways of outwitting everyone and win. And because you have access to the same suppliers as every other dropshipper on the internet, the only place where any competition really exists is in attracting customers to your store rather than your competitor's.

More importantly, you have to keep tabs on the competition. This way, you will catch any new innovations in your category and position yourself as the second entrant, if not the first. In fact, some economics scholars argue that the second entrant has the best position because the rest of the market is always trying to beat the first entrant. Anyway, without much further ado, let's look at the exact strategies you can employ at your store to spy on your competitors.

Shopify

The first thing to competing is knowing who you are competing against. It is virtually impossible to scour the selling pages of Shopify, and other marketplaces to find out what dropshippers are selling the same products as you. However, with the right skills, you can indeed identify what Shopify stores are your competitors. A simple Google search of **site:myshopify.com"keyword"** (whereby the keyword is a word that best describes your store) will bring up a complete list of competitors for you to start keeping tabs on.

To approximate how much your competitor is selling, you can sacrifice a few dollars to buy the cheapest product on their store. Note down the order number for that purchase. After one month, buy again and check the new order number. The difference between the two orders represents the number of orders the store has handled in the past one month.

Another trick to competing on Shopify is the Diamond SKU, a top-selling product that a store owner opts to keep off their shop because they are afraid of being copied. Instead, they sell on the Shopify marketplace and their own private marketing channels.

To find out if your category has any Diamond SKU's, add **/collections/all?sort_by=best-selling.** This trick tells you not just what products are selling well on Shopify but also the prices the sellers are charging for them.

BuiltWith

BuiltWith is a tracking services company that enables web developers and designers to identify the technologies that other websites are using. It is free on Shopify, even though it comes in handy when you don't want to miss out on new technologies your competition is using to get ahead. Using BuiltWith is simply a matter of inserting a competitor's name on a search bar in BuiltWith.com. The tools you can identify with BuiltWith include widgets, analytical tools, CDNs, payment gateways, email hosting, and server technology. With this information at hand, you can determine the best tools to add to your store yourself to gain an edge.

Mention

Mention alerts you whenever your store is mentioned in social media or in a blog article. It is a wonderful analytical tool that lets you keep track of your store and monitor the effectiveness of your marketing efforts. The trick is, you can use Mention to keep tabs on your competitors as well. Mention lets you set the alerts you receive about a competitor's activities including their customer engagements. Any time an alert brings to your attention an unfavorable mention by a customer is an opportunity you get to swoop in and offer them better terms and poach them off.

By adding exclusion terms to the search results, you can eliminate the Shopify store completely and identify other sales channels your competitor is using and how they are promoting their products. With this information at hand, you then max out your advertising and start taking customers away from them, gradually nudging them off the competitors' list. To this end, Mention enables you to identify influential social media personalities whom you can approach and forge strong relationships, collaborating on affiliate marketing for your mutual benefit.

AHREFS

Ahrefs uses bots and a database of search page results from trillions of website connections to bring you link research utilities like e-commerce backlink research on your competitor's store. With Ahrefs, you can find out precisely why store you compete with on Shopify ranks higher than you on the search results.

You simply enter their URL on the search tab and run a search to get results on the keywords the store is using, their pay-per-click ads budget (if any), and the results of these efforts. With this information, you can endeavor to make improvements on your own store and hopefully rank as highly as they.

Fadfeed

Fadfeed is the ultimate spying tool for Facebook ad traffic. The tool comes as a free Chrome browser extension that opens you up to a world of ads in as many categories as you would like to view. By modifying the search words, you can find out exactly what strategies your competitors are using to attract buyers through Facebook. Any effective strategies you see being used by a competitor is fair game for you to mimic and use on your store.

10 Ways to Beat the Competition and Win in Your Dropshipping Business

As mentioned above, dropshipping is all about outwitting your competitors for a limited market using marketing and targeting strategies. Below is a list of 10 things I have discovered to work very well in making your Shopify store highly profitable.

1. Give your customers the option to call you. Adding a phone number to your website along with the email address and social media pages allows you to establish a better relationship with your customers. Giving your number to the site visitors indicates courage, openness, and willingness to communicate. You will be surprised when you receive calls that go like, "I wanted to make sure that you are a legit business first."

2. On the point above, **always return missed calls.** Nothing annoys people more than calling (maybe even twice or more) when you have a really pressing issue and the person never called you back. Return all calls no matter where you are and as soon as you can.

3. Use add-ons like privy exit intent on your website. People visit your store and, for one reason or another, leave without making an order. With privy exit intent, you make a last-ditch attempt to get the visitor to commit to a future purchase by asking for their contact details. The most common method of

taking a visitor's details so that you can keep enticing them to buy is to offer them a coupon of, say 10%, that you are to send via email. Few people can resist the temptation of a free gift. If you make a 7- or 14-day coupon or give whatever duration to it, the visitor is even more likely to buy.

4. Bonus gifts are not nearly as common as they should be in the highly competitive world of dropshipping. Bonus gifts attract new buyers and allow you to build your brand recognition.

5. Get your suppliers to review your store. When customers visit your site and see reviews of your work by reputable suppliers, they will be more impressed, more confident in your ability to deliver, and more inclined to buy.

6. The Shopify app allows for communication between visitors and you as the host via the Tidio Live Chat. To make sure that you are always reachable, you can download Tidio on your phone and respond to every chat left by visitors to your store.

7. Offers. Offers. Offers. Humans are motivated by fear and greed above all other emotions when making a purchase decision. You can exploit these emotions on your store by giving expiring offers with countdown clocks to urge visitors to buy now before the discount expires. This way, you sell more products and make money from volume sales. Scarcity elicits feelings of fear, prompting visitors to buy even when they had

not initially planned to buy now. Phrases like "offer valid while stock lasts" go a long way in convincing unsure buyer to click on the **Add to Cart** button. Inventory countdowns to show how much you are selling while a product is on offer increases your conversion rate because more visitors are persuaded to buy.

8. Be ready to pivot. Pivoting allows you to adjust your MO to exploit a niche product or market, expand suddenly because demand spikes suddenly, or add new trending products to rejuvenate slumping sales. Never settle into the comfort zone, even when your store becomes more popular than you'd ever imagined.

9. Provide your visitors with unique content. Buyers like to think that they have just made an informed decision. They scour through tons of blogs and will unconsciously trust the seller who helped them make their purchase decision. A blog sets you aside from the hoi polloi as a knowledgeable seller who can take the customer's hand and guide them in the journey to making the decision to buy.

10. Be active on your store every day, but take time for your own relaxation. The perfect balance when running an e-commerce store is between full-time availability to your customers and having time to yourself. Set aside time to respond to messages and orders (about 2 hours). In this time, you work on your store full-time. For the next four to six hours, you can be available to reply to messages, talk with suppliers,

etc. two hours before and after sleep is your sanctuary time to rewind.

Many dropshippers make the mistake of making the business their whole life. Working around the clock does not make you a better dropshipper. Smart work beats hard work at any time of the day.

Pro Tip 11: Keep an eye on the competition. Spy on them, copy their moves, jump into trends, and follow the currents, but only when you are learning. After learning everything you need to know about dropshipping, you can start setting your own trends and doing your own thing.

Chapter 11: Marketing to Scale Up

Every business needs a good marketing strategy to work. When you start out, virtually no one knows about your business, the products you offer, and your terms. Before customers can start buying from you, it is important that you start reaching out to them, making them aware of your business. In this chapter, we shall look at the different avenues where you can reach out to people willing to pay for your products and the strategies that you can use to do so.

When deciding to start advertising on either of these channels, you should consider the money you intend to use in your marketing efforts. You can then evaluate each advertisement medium and allocate a portion of your total budget based on its effectiveness. Starting out, a daily budget of about $10 spread between Facebook, Pinterest, is recommended. Henceforth, you can increase the budget on each platform based on the results of each post.

Facebook

Facebook makes for such a great starting point for your marketing campaign because it is home to 1.23 billion active users. Facebook allows you to use organic as well as paid methods of promoting your store. If you start a Facebook page and share it with your friends, you will get some attention for the products you are selling, probably even manage to squeeze a sale. However, the organic method of marketing on Facebook can only go far. You will need to up the ante with paid advertisements.

Paid ads on Facebook fall into three stages. We have campaigns, ad sets, and ads. At the campaign stage, you establish the main goal of the advertisements. With your Shopify store, you can decide to have ads for the entire website promoting your brand and another promoting the individual products or a select listing of your products to encourage purchases.

Ad setting entails tailoring your advertisements to a very specific demographic. At this point, you have started targeting the people you think are more likely to buy what you are selling. Before embarking on this step, you should sit down and write a very detailed profile of the perfect customer, namely the people you should be targeting with your adverts. Use the Facebook Audience Insights tool to sort the right audience by age, gender, geographic location, occupation, the groups they belong to on Facebook, and interests.

Finally, you design the ad itself. You must think of the message you want to pass along, the senses you want to appeal to, as well as the emotions you want to invoke. Think of the medium: a video, a photo, or just text? Depending on the product you are selling and the people you are targeting, you should pick the graphic that will appeal best to their specific characteristics. If you don't have the skills to create the kind of ad you want, consider hiring freelance graphic designers for the task. They are available on freelance websites like Fiverr for as little as $5.

Instagram

Selling on Instagram is not much different from selling on Facebook. The main difference emerges in the way you post the ad. With Facebook, you can post an ad without linking to a page on Facebook. Anyone who clicks on your ad will then be taken straight to your website. With Instagram, the rules are a little different.

When you advertise on Instagram, you simply put up a normal post, then boost it to make it visible to more users. On the whole, Instagram is less effective as a medium for advertisements in the category of self-posted promotional content.

However, Instagram makes up for this ineffectiveness with a different kind of advertisement potential: influencers. Big brands have been using celebrity product ambassadors to drive demand. With Instagram influencers, even your tiny business can tap into the influencer marketing potential.

Pinterest

Not only is Pinterest handy for finding the right products to stock on your website, but it also allows you to promote your business to users on the site. By creating viral content and sharing with your network, you can set off a sharing chain of events that could generate massive sales for your shop. The rule with Pinterest, just as with any other social networking site, is to create content that promotes your products but is also interesting and fun so that people can share widely.

With Pinterest, you can create another shop where people can come and view the products you dropship, the benefits, descriptions, and price just as easily as they would on your store. You should link every product to your Shopify store, enabling viewers to link directly into the store should they want to buy from you.

Google

The Google network is a vast universe that spans desktop and mobile websites, applications, and search engines. With Google, you don't just advertise blindly, you keep track of every impression generated by the advert in the form of pay per click. This is a major advantage over the likes of Facebook, Instagram, and others where you can never be sure if the money you spent translated to tangible results.

Google allows you to target a specific market and keep a tally of the exact number of people who clicked on your ad. This comes in handy while calculating for conversion rates to determine how much interest your products are generating among the people who view them. Another thing about Google is that it ranks ads based on their quality and the quality of the webpage they advertise. The more professional both look, the higher the rank you will have, and the greater the impact your ads will have. Just keep in mind that ad rank is something you build over time as you constantly improve both the quality of your ads and your store.

Email Marketing

In chapter 11, we touched on the idea of enticing people to sign on to your mailing list with coupons and discounts. An email list is one of the oldest but most effective marketing tools available for the dropshipper. The great thing about email marketing is that it is highly targeted, cheap, and effective.

Email marketing at the website when you set up the Privy Exit Intent addon. You can then decide how much discount to attach to it to entice every visitor to your website to submit their email address for "special emails on deals, discounts, and offers."

With the email list, you can be more proactive because you can be almost sure that the ads will be received and read. However, you should respect the users' privacy and only send emails to those who agreed to receive them. If a customer unsubscribes, count that as a small loss and work harder to replace them with ten more subscribers.

Twitter

Twitter comes in very handy in helping you boost your brand. While the rest of the resources discussed here allow users to market the old way by taking promotional messages to potential customers, Twitter focuses on brand identity management. With the platform, you get the opportunity to personalize your store and give it a real relatable identity. The marketing you do on Twitter masquerades as conversations with a devoted audience.

However, you can still run a campaign on Twitter, promoting your conversations and posts to reach more people and make a better impression. The Twitter advertising interface is very particular. You must start by selecting an objective for the campaign, either engagements on Twitter, website clicks or conversions (you must share an HTML link with this type of ad), followers on Twitter, or leads. At one time or another, you will run an ad using either one of these metrics. Over time, you will need to increase followers, generate greater engagement on your tweets, send people to your website to buy, and generate leads. Twitter also has a very detailed analytics tool that enables you to track the impact of your advertisement.

YouTube Marketing

Video advertisements have a massive advantage over other types of ads in that they immerse the viewer into the product experience much better. Studies have shown that customers are more likely to buy a product after watching a product video.

And it doesn't have to be that long a video — even the short 30-second videos accomplish more than a picture ever can because it shows the product in a more relatable way. In dropshipping — where the customer buys products even without seeing them — the realism created by a video goes a long way in boosting conversion rates.

Retargeting Customers

Visitors rarely buy on their first visit to your store. The vast majority of buyers do so after a false start or two. To ensure that people who visit your store and leave without buying anything come back and actually buy something, we use a strategy known as retargeting. With retargeting, you place a tracking pixel that follows bounced visitors in other websites, keeping your brand and/or product in view to try and persuade them to return and hopefully make a purchase this time.

When retargeting, you should only go after visitors whose actions within your website were promising. A visitor who put items in the cart but did not check them out would need much less persuasion to actually buy than one who came in, read a blog article or two, then exited. Place your ad in front of the former. You should also ensure that the retargeting ad should follow the bounced buyer immediately they leave your store. It is during this time that they are more likely to come back and buy.

How to Make the Business More Passive

Running an online store can be very tasking work. However, with automatic tools, your store can very efficiently run itself while you go on holiday, sleep, or just hang. Automation is the name of the game when it comes to passive income in dropshipping. The more the processes of the dropshipping process you can automate, the more effectively your store will be able to run on its own.

The first choice for automation is to use dropshipping automation tools like Around.io, Aftership, Watchlyst, and Beeketing. They take care of different steps of the dropshipping process. The only downside is that they are not 100% dependable. They could experience a glitch that would paralyze your whole business.

The second choice is to hire a programmer to write you a custom-build application to take care of all your needs. You can look for these professionals in dropshipping communities are full of programmers with nifty little tools who can help you go fully automatic. Alternatively, you can visit freelancing websites like Freelancer, Upwork, Guru, and Fiverr. They also have programming experts in abundance. All you have to do is post your project and invite professionals to bid. Just be sure to make the freelancer sign a non-disclosure agreement to protect your secrets.

Seasonal Items

When dealing with seasonal items, the early bird catches the worm. You can start building momentum as the season approaches by posting ads in the marketplace. At this point, you capture the early movers market. As you continue selling and advertising long before the rest of the market catches on, you will boost your SEO ranking so that when the season of frenzied buying actually comes around, your ads will feature higher than other sellers'.

Pro Tip 12: Marketing strategies work. It is important to take your store and products in it to the market. This can only be done by running an aggressive promotions strategy.

Chapter 12: Personal Branding

Personal branding refers to the process of building a distinct identity for a person. It allows you to take charge of your public image, molding you into a leader and influencer in your selected niche. With personal branding, your identity becomes an asset that you can use to advance yourself. In dropshipping, your personal brand will bring more credibility for your business identity and help you to sell more products. While some people settle for business brands exclusively in their marketing mix, the current age of social media demands for a more relatable brand. A person is loads more relatable than a business can ever be.

Personal branding is vital for success in dropshipping for the reason that it gives the business owner (and the business in extension) more authority in the category. In a world where perfectionism is valued beyond anything else, creating the perception of flawlessness goes a long way. However, rather than be a hollow vessel, it is also good to back it up with some real skills.

Why Create a Brand

A personal brand is not a very easy thing to accomplish. It calls for you to maintain a consistent behavioral pattern for a long time. The qualities of a strong personal brand that come in very handy in running a dropshipping business include:

Authenticity

A good brand stands out from the rest, exploiting small differences between the individual and "the rest" to convince the public that they are getting something special.

Reliability

Money does not always motivate people. Sometimes, a business person won't mind that their action affects their margin if it happens for a short time. However, the personal brand — as a marketing tool that is essentially you — would be greatly affected if you acted in a manner not considered right. Customers will trust a Shopify store run by a strong personal brand because they are quite certain that the operator will want to maintain a good reputation to protect their personal brand.

Tactics for Creating a Strong Brand

A strong brand does not just happen. It is formed through a series of very deliberate actions as explained below:

1. Formulate a personal branding statement

The branding statement allows you to define the audience for whom the identity is created and other brands in competition with you.

2. Use social media for communication purposes

You start working on your desired image by using social media to communicate your brand message.

3. Monitor the brand

Your personal brand should be an identity that remains steady and reliable not just for the target audience but also for the business and for you. Any changes must be well-considered and incorporated into the brand as subtly as possible.

Benefits of Personal Branding in Dropshipping

When starting your dropshipping business, any momentum is always a good thing to have. Momentum often comes from the personal identity of the founder.

To be specific, it inspires the customers' confidence and trust. After years of perceived greed and exploitation, the general public has come to destruct big business with a passion. However, it does not mean that people trust a new and untested business. With a strong personal brand of the owner, customers will be more willing to try it out.

A personal brand establishes you as a leader in a certain area. This sets your business apart as the go-to for establishment for the best products in the category.

Pro Tip 13: A strong brand is an invaluable asset for a dropshipping business. The brand takes on a greater role than the business and the products you sell. A good brand pushes demand and establishes your dropshipping business into a profitable outfit.

Chapter 13: Mistakes to Avoid

Here is an interesting fact: 90% of startup dropshipping businesses fail within one month of starting operations. The founders give up within the first few months of starting out, which means that they end up missing out on a great opportunity to earn passive income. This chapter discusses the reasons why dropshipping businesses fail and highlights ways through which you can avoid falling into the trap.

Selecting the Wrong Niche

If you choose a niche that is already crowded or one that is not sustainable (not enough demand to support an entire business), you will probably end in failure. To avoid falling into this pitfall, conduct proper research on the niche and ensure that you run a test run before committing all your resources to the business

Impatience

Because of the numerous stories detailing the almost overnight success of people who entered into dropshipping, people expect that it will be easy to start a profitable business. When the expected success does not come soon enough, people give up. The solution is to recognize that dropshipping takes hard work and time to reward investors with profits. Giving up halfway through is rather self-defeating.

Lack of Capital

Again, the reputation of dropshipping as the ultimate investment conspires to screw a lot of beginners out of a great opportunity to make money. Dropshipping is not a business you can start with zero investment as some people would have you believe. The fix for this mistake is to set aside a small kitty to use in establishing your online store.

Bad Marketing

Depending on the product you sell, the platforms discussed in chapter 12 can either work or flop miserably. To determine the best platform, conduct a test run and determine what platform has the best return on investment.

Settling for Expensive Products From a Single Supplier

The thing to keep in mind is that you can only raise the price of a product so high. When you get a product at the store price, you can hardly upsell it and make a profit. Ensure that you get bargain prices for every product you buy so that even after adding the margin, your price is still low enough to be competitive.

Poor Customer Service

If you don't take good care of your customers, they will go to businesses that do. Communication is especially very important to avoid frayed nerves. Ensure that you provide your customers with sufficient customer care attendants.

Delays

Because the dropshipper does not make any shipment, it falls entirely up to your business' supplier. Unforeseen and uncommunicated delays lead to product cancellation, suspension, and losses. Select your supplier well to make sure that they fulfill orders within time.

Inconsistencies and Absenteeism

Dropshipping requires a level of consistency and total dedication to take off. Failure to dedicate enough time to take care of the business before it takes off would lead to failed stores. The solution is very simple: be prepared to go the stretch even if there are numerous challenges ahead. Don't give up or run away just because your new business is going through.

Poor Choice of Website Design

The website you use for your store must be well-designed and optimized for selling. New dropshippers make the mistake of leaving their websites drab and boring possibly because of the whole "zero investment" idea. Better-designed businesses win all the customers you would have sold to. It is critical to optimize your website for selling.

Ridiculous Expectations

I will blame the hype for this one, too. Most new sellers come to dropshipping believing that they will be making $10,000 in extra income every month within no time. When this does not happen, the disappointment is too crushing and they give up. Expect to toil for every dollar and forget the whole zero-investment concept. It is unreal and grossly misleading.

Failing to Plan for Marketing

A marketing plan is critical for success in dropshipping. It allows you to reach out to prospective buyers and make them buyers for real. When you don't plan what platforms to use, you will probably waste all your money and get no tangible results. The solution: write a detailed marketing plan beforehand.

Failing to Diversify

Just because you have found a good niche product and survived for a year now in the jungle of dropshipping, it does not mean that your business is sustainable. The cliché "putting all your eggs in one basket" applies here. Try and start a few stores on Shopify and let them fight it out in the field.

Ignoring SEO

SEO is one of the most important marketing tools available for dropshippers on the internet. It is used by Google to rank search results. To avoid being the last result that comes on every Google search, optimize all your product listings for keyword recognition.

Ignoring Regulations

From licenses to permits, business registration, and copyright filing, dropshippers have to jump through puddles to become legitimately operating companies. It is impossible to expand without these documents, so instead of blocking your own success just register, acquire permits, and pay all your taxes.

Chapter 14: Dropshipping Hacks

I believe that I have taught you everything there is to know about dropshipping. As you prepare to start using this information to practical use, let me add something more to it: a list of tricks you can use to make your store profitable beyond your wildest dreams.

Split Variants

When you are highly focused on a single niche like beauty or electronics, you will have products in your store that are the same but with different features. Split these variants into diverse products to increase exposure for each. You can do this via the Oberlo App by simply clicking on the **Split Product** tab. Sure, you give yourself extra work writing new descriptions, but your store becomes so saturated with the product that your SEO rank rises substantially. All your products will also be visible, so visitors will have a much better variety to pick from.

Sell on AliExpress

AliExpress is a sales channel that can add some traffic to your website and possibly bring in some buying customers as well. When dropshipping on Shopify, Oberlo is the tool you use to import products into your store. You can add AliExpress to your store as a sales channel just like we have discussed.

Let Customers Track Their Order on Backend

There are lots of challenges to buying something online, but none can be quite as irksome as waiting. You buy something you are really excited about, pay for it, but have to wait for a few hours (if you are lucky) or days (the most likely scenario) before taking possession of it. You will get a lot of customers bombarding you with questions about when their order will be arriving at their doorstep. It gets somehow awkward answering these questions because you are not really doing the shipping. With Backend, you share the tracking details the supplier gave you and allow the customer to follow their order as it moves from the warehouse to their home.

Choose ePacket

No other supplier offers a shipping package that is as cheap and as quick as the one offered by ePacket. With shipping costs averaging below $5, ePacket allows you to get magnanimous, especially when you are dealing with products with higher prices, higher margins, and better profits. ePacket also delivers its packages within one week at the most. If you want to crush the shipping process and don't want to break open your bank account to do it, the ePacket is the way to go.

Use the Customer's Preferred Method of Paying

Buyers on Shopify must give their payment details to shop. Sellers also have to submit their payment details with Shopify, as we discussed in chapter 4. Most users have PayPal as their preferred way to pay because it is easy, secure, and available in over 200 regions. However, not every customer will have a payment system that matches one of yours. Instead of watching them walk away with their money, use Shopify Payments to take their payments in whatever system they are submitting it on. Shopify Payments allows customers to pay in their chosen way rather than making the transaction about you receiving money from them.

Take Shopify With You Wherever You Go

The **Buy** button on Shopify is a very dynamic feature. You can insert it on any website you are an admin of, giving visitors access to the products cart and secure checkout anywhere you go. Basically, you open as many counters in as many platforms as you want and all of them are linked together in the master-store at Shopify. So, if you have been blogging on Squarespace, Tumblr, or WordPress prior to starting your Shopify store, you can take advantage of the customer base accumulated there to boost sales on the latter.

Override a Supplier

There are many reasons why you may need to change the supplier on a particular product. You can be dissatisfied with their services or simply be replacing a supplier who has run out of a product with one who still has it in stock. Anyway, there is an easy way to do this from your Shopify store without removing the product from the page. You merely have to click on the **Override This Product** button on the **Action** tab and insert a link to the new supplier.

Use Facebook Demo Ads

Demo ads are very effective as a promotional tool. Not only do they double up as a user guide, but it is also easier to convince a prospective buyer to become a customer after viewing a demo video. After all, it shows them exactly how handy the product will be should they decide to buy it. Video ads are more effective than any other media when it comes to advertisements.

Change Ad Budgets After Midnight

Any advertisement money you spend — whether on Facebook, Twitter, Instagram, or Google — is spent throughout the day. When you decide to take it up a notch with more expenditure in the middle of the day, you force the ad placement algorithms to go wild trying to figure out places to send your ads to spend the updated daily budget. The data you collect on the first day (the most important day of any campaign) thus becomes inefficient and may cause you to change your mind about the whole campaign.

Disrupt the Category

In the world of business, changes affect everyone in an industry one of two ways; you make a bunch of money or you go out of business. The same idea applies for dropshipping. You and the stores that you compete with on your category make up the industry. The market is usually at ease when no one is doing anything to take it over. However, if you take it easy and settle into the status quo, you will get disrupted at one point. The market will be whipped from right under your feet and you will be left in the cold as the disruptor reaps the benefits of disrupting the market. Endeavor to be the disruptor and be constantly on the lookout for the silver bullet that will give you total dominance over the category. If you don't, someone else will... ultimately.

Conclusion

The future of the world is digital — this much is clear. Pretty much everything is going online now — government services, interpersonal interactions, and commerce, to name a few. The internet is great for a number of reasons, but the greatest one is that it gives power to the masses to operate as they will. Nowhere has this phenomenon been clear than in dropshipping. Hundreds of thousands of online stores are operated by enterprising individuals on the internet, using basic supply and demand concepts to simplify an otherwise knotty landscape of international trade.

Through dropshipping, international borders are taken out of the equation when buying something. International shipping means that Chinese products don't necessarily come in bulk on board some massive ships at the shore. A single consumer in a small town somewhere in Nebraska can order for a single product from a New York merchant and have it delivered by a supplier from Shenzhen.

It is easy to join this exciting new space, but you will have to adhere to a certain set of rules to become a successful dropshipper. You must hone your entrepreneurial skills and approach dropshipping with a singular desire to not just win but to win decisively. So, other than the technical aspects of it, don't try too hard to learn how to become a dropshipper. That is just what you do, not who you are. Success in this field will only come by cultivating the more dynamic character of an entrepreneur.

From the times of Carnegie and Rockefeller to the modern times of Zuckerberg and Branson, entrepreneurs have shaped the way we do things not just in their chosen field but in the whole world as well. Now, that is something! It may seem like a big deal to aspire to, but why not just start with that product category and then move up from there?

Printed in Great Britain
by Amazon